The Thrush

A thrush sits in a nest.
The nest is in a tall shrub.
The thrush sits on six eggs.

1

A cat comes by.
It is Gus.
The thrush gets mad.
She yells at Gus,
"Stop, cat, stop!"
It is a shrill yell.

Gus does not stop.
He comes up to the shrub.
He begins to jump
to a branch.

The thrush must stop Gus.
She must not let him
get her eggs.
The mother thrush zips
off her nest.

Gus runs after the thrush.
The thrush zips by Mac,
the dog.

Mac sees Gus run.
Mac runs after Gus.
It is tag!

Gus jumps on top of the van.
Mac sits by the van
and yips at Gus.

The thrush is glad
Gus is on the van.
The thrush is glad Mac
yips at Gus.
She grins and goes back
to her nest.

Shrimp for Gus?

Gus, the cat, sees a bag
by the shrubs.

He can smell the bag.
What is in the bag?
He can smell shrimp!
He can smell crabs!

Gus grabs the bag.
He thrusts his chin
into the bag.
Where are the shrimp?
Where are the crabs?

Gus hunts for the shrimp.
He sniffs and sniffs.
He can smell
shrimp and crabs,
but he cannot see them.

Gus flips and rips the bag.
He begins to shred it.
The cat is mad.
He says, "This bag had
shrimp and crabs in it.
Who got my shrimp
and crabs?"

A thrush lands on the shrub.
She mocks Gus
with a shrill call.
She calls, "That is just trash!
No shrimp or crabs for you!"

Gus is mad at the thrush.
He wants crab and shrimp.
But he drops the bag
that is trash.
Then he walks back
to his bench in the sun.

Six Friends

Sam has the ball.
Rick and Scott have the bats.
Kim, Pam, and Jill have
the mats.
They set the mats
on the grass.

16

Sam thrusts his hand
into his mitt.
So do Rick and Scott.
Rick goes out to the grass
with Scott.

Sam pitches the ball
to Kim.
Wham! Kim gets a hit.

The ball goes past
the shrubs.
It goes past the benches.
It goes all the way
to the pond.

Kim runs fast to all the mats.
"What a thrill!" she tells Pam.
"We will win."

Sam pitches the ball to Pam.
Pam hits the ball.
Whack!
The ball goes up and up
and up.

Scott and Rick both run
for the ball.
Rick yells, "I will get it!"
He thrusts his mitt up.
Rick grabs the pop-up ball.

What a thrill!
"Pam is out," says Rick.
"They will not win.
We will win."

The sun is hot.
The grass is soft.
The friends pitch and catch
and bat and run.
Who will win?